Written by: Cindy Fish
Illustrated by: Lydia Varnum

Dedicated to: The Campetella Family

Thank you for sharing PARTY prayer with us. The revival in Palm Coast in 2022 changed our family forever.

PARTY PRAYER

Written by: Cindy Fish
Illustrated by: Lydia Varnum

An imprint of Truth Book Company, LLC
Anderson, IN

Printed in the United States of America
ISBN: 978-1-965584-22-4, paperback
ISBN: 978-1-965584-23-1 hardcover

For information about special discounts,
bulk purchases, or hosting a live event,
please visit www.truthbook.co

you're invited!

PARTY PRAYER

author:
CINDY FISH

illustrator:
LYDIA VARNUM

you're invited!

to a very special place.
A place we meet Jesus,
face to face.

It's not the usual
party with balloons
or ice cream that melts...

But it's a place where
God's presence can be felt.
cake
tent
rest
alter

It's a place we can run to,
a place we can hide.

It's always a party
with Jesus by our side.

"We hope you'll join the fun. When you start to pray, the party's just begun!"

anyone

who

anytime

when

anywhere

where

It's called PARTY prayer,
each letter is a clue...

To help you learn just
what you should do!

wisdom
good
ness
peace
Heal
ing
hope
LOVE
PRO
PHECY
JOY

We'll open up gifts like
peace, patience and joy.
What we get from Jesus is
better than any toy.

Are you ready? Yay! Come right in!
Clear your mind and let's begin.

...is for

PRAISE

We lift our voice and
our hands we raise.

We clap & shout,
HALLELUJAH
You're worthy of all
PRAISE!

"You're wonderful, powerful, you're all things true.
Jesus, we'll never get tired of praising you."

"You're holy, you're good, my Father above.
I just can't stop shouting all about your love!"

...is for
ASK

We bring to Him every problem, every need.

There's nothing too big or too small to plead.

When you're sick or hurt
or feeling afraid,
you can ask Jesus,
He's never delayed.

"I ask in faith and
trust Your way,
knowing You hear me
every time that I pray."

"Please touch my family and save my friends. I ask everything...

NAME,

AMEN.

...is for
REPENT

Sometimes we mess up
and disobey,
but Jesus is faithful
to forgive
when we choose to
change and turn away.

"I'm sorry, Lord,
forgive me of my sin.

I want to live for you
and never sin again."

"Make my heart clean
and brand-new inside.
Fill me with Your Spirit,
come in and abide."

When we turn from sin, we
start fresh and new—
That's what repentance
& the Holy Ghost will do!

...is for
THANKS

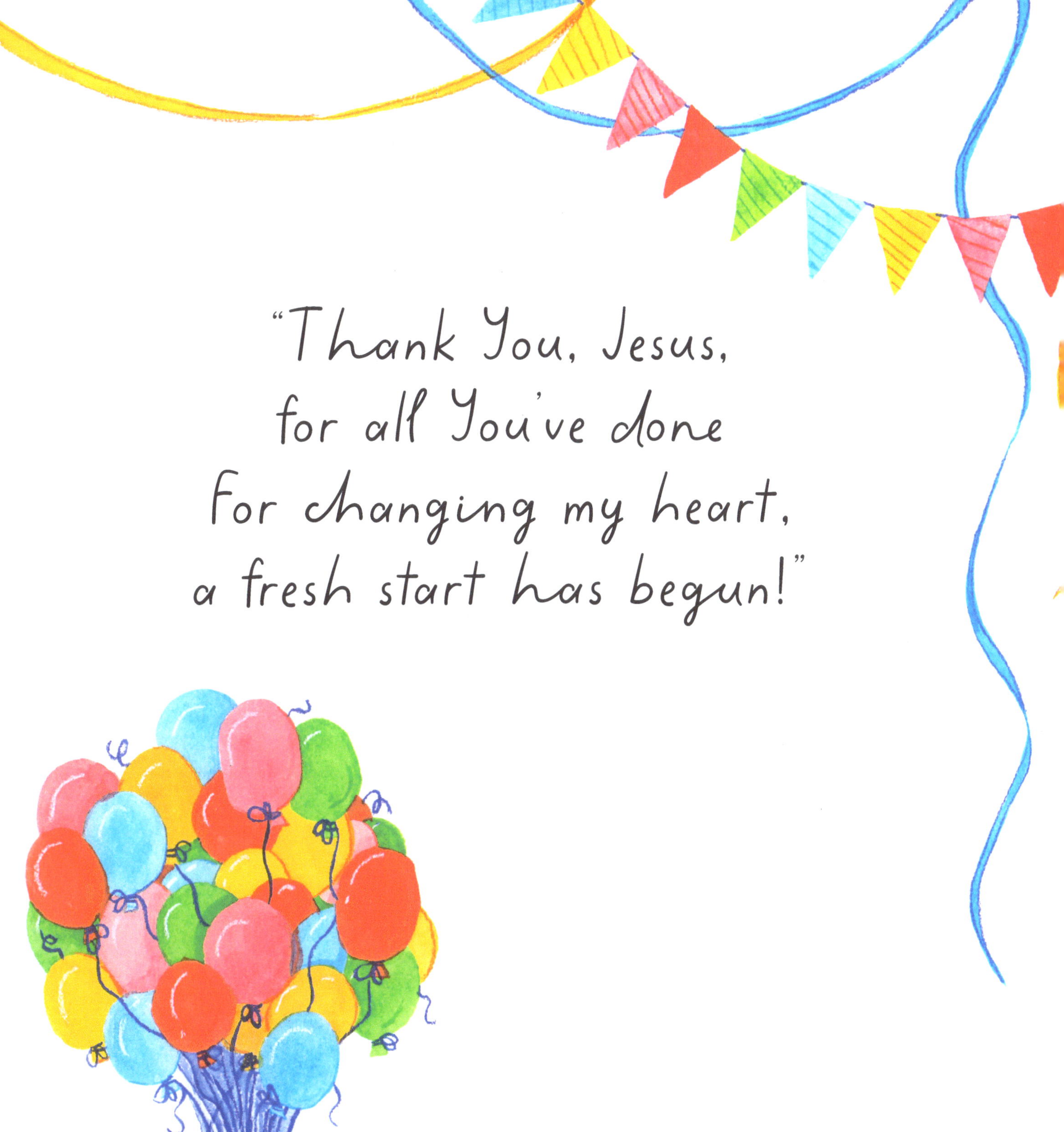

"Thank You, Jesus,
for all You've done
For changing my heart,
a fresh start has begun!"

"Thank You for my pastor,
thank You for my home,
Thank You, Jesus,
that I'm never alone."

"Thank you for healing me.
Thank you for protection.
Thank you for all of your
love and affection."

...is for

YIELD

Now it's time to wait and hear.
Jesus is close. His voice is near.

There's something special
He wants you to do...

And while you are praying;
He may just tell you!

"Not my will, but Yours each day.
Speak to my heart, God,
show me the way."

"I'll go anywhere,
I'll do all you ask.
I won't be afraid no
matter the task."

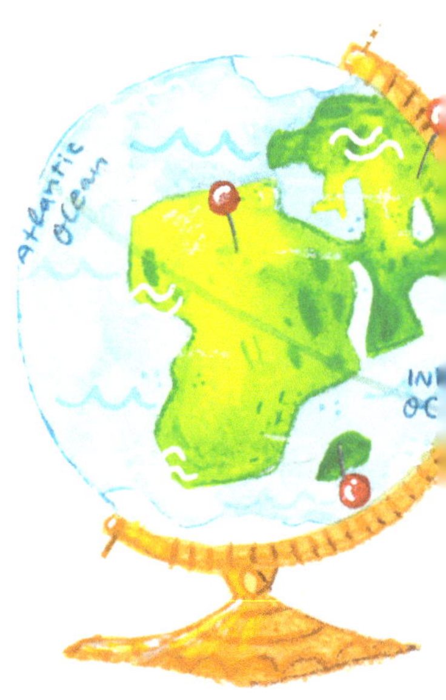

Sometimes you'll whisper.
Sometimes you'll cry.

Sometimes the Spirit
comes rushing by.

Your tongue might speak a language you don't understand...

that's the Holy Ghost, just like He planned!

It happened in Acts,
it can happen for you.
This gift is a promise,
He'll fill you too!

He's your Creator,
your Savior,
your very best friend!

Pray without ceasing,
and the party won't end.

Tomorrow is waiting,
so please don't delay...

I love you JESUS
Let's PARTY with Jesus every single day!
thank you for your GOODNESS today God!

P "Let everything that has breath praise the Lord! Praise the Lord!" (Psalm 150:6 ESV)

A "Ask, and it will be given to you; seek, and you will find; knock, and it will be opened to you." (Matthew 7:7 ESV)

R "If we confess our sins, he is faithful and just to forgive us our sins and to cleanse us from all unrighteousness." (1 John 1:9 ESV)

T "give thanks in all circumstances; for this is the will of God in Christ Jesus for you." (1 Thessalonians 5:18 ESV)

Y "saying, "Father, if you are willing, remove this cup from me. Nevertheless, not my will, but yours, be done." (Luke 22:42 ESV)

"And they were all filled
with the Holy Spirit and
began to speak in other
tongues as the Spirit gave
them utterance."

–Acts 2:4 (ESV)

Let's have a Prayer PARTY

Jesus, I PRAISE you for...

Jesus, I ASK you to help me with...

Jesus, I REPENT for...

Jesus, THANK you for...

Jesus, today I YIELD...

In Jesus Name I pray, Amen.

Explore more titles from
Truth Book Company at
www.truthbook.co

www.ingramcontent.com/pod-product-compliance
Lightning Source LLC
LaVergne TN
LVHW070221110826
845147LV00003B/616

* 9 7 8 1 9 6 5 5 8 4 2 2 4 *